Knights and Castles

By Rupert Matthews

Series Editor Deborah Lock
Editor Radhika Haswani
Senior Art Editor Ann Cannings
Art Editor Kanika Kalra
Producer, Pre-production Nadine King
Picture Researcher Sakshi Saluja
DTP Designers Neeraj Bhatia, Dheeraj Singh
Managing Editor Soma B. Chowdhury
Art Director Martin Wilson

Reading Consultant
Linda Gambrell, Ph.D.

First published in Great Britain in 2016
by Dorling Kindersley Limited
80 Strand, London, WC2R 0RL

A CIP catalogue record for this book
is available from the British Library
ISBN: 978-0-2412-5762-3

Printed and bound in China.

The publisher would like to thank the following for their kind permission to reproduce their photographs:
(Key: a-above; b-below/bottom; c-centre; f-far; l-left; r-right; t-top)

3 **Dorling Kindersley:** Wallace Collection, London (r, bc). 4 **Dreamstime.com:** Maaridi (t). 5 **Alamy Images:**
Michael Morrison. 6-7 **Dorling Kindersley:** Dave Rudkin / Gordon Models - modelmaker. 8-9 **Dorling Kindersley:**
Dave Rudkin / Gordon Models - modelmaker. 10 **Dreamstime.com:** Sandesh Patil (cb). 12-13 **Dreamstime.com:**
Severija (t); Veremer. 14 **Dreamstime.com:** Maaridi (t). 17 **Fotolia:** Derya Celik (cb). 20-21 **Corbis:** Charles
Bowman / robertharding. 22-23 **Dreamstime.com:** Severija (t). 22 **Dreamstime.com:** Tupungato (crb).
23 **Dreamstime.com:** Michele Stefanile / Zorin (cr). 24-25 **Dreamstime.com:** Severija (t). 26 **Dreamstime.com:**
Maaridi (t). 27 **Corbis:** Max Milligan / JAI. 29 **By permission of The British Library.** 30 **Corbis:** Alinari
Archives. 33 **Corbis:** Tarker. 34-35 **Dreamstime.com:** Severija (t). 34 **Getty Images:** Universal History Archive
(tc). 35 **Alamy Images:** 19th era 2 (tc). 36 **Getty Images:** Universal History Archive (c). 36-37 **Dreamstime.com:**
Claudiodivizia; Severija (t). 38 **Dreamstime.com:** Maaridi (t). 40-41 **Getty Images:** PHAS. 41 **Dreamstime.com:**
Sandesh Patil (tr). 42-43 **Corbis:** Tibor Bognar. 44 **Dreamstime.com:** Sandesh Patil (tr). 44-45 **Getty Images:**
PHAS (b). 46 **Dreamstime.com:** Theo Malings / Theohrm (ca). 46-47 **123RF.com:** Nathanael005.
Dorling Kindersley: Wallace Collection, London (b). **Dreamstime.com:** Severija (t). 48 **Dreamstime.com:** Maaridi
(t). 49 **Fotolia:** Derya Celik (ca). 50-51 **Alamy Images:** The Art Archive. 52 **Getty Images:** Stock Montage (tr).
52-53 **Getty Images:** Peter Thompson / Heritage Images (b). 54-55 **Corbis:** Steven Vidler / Eurasia Press.
56-57 **Dreamstime.com:** Severija (t). 57 **Alamy Images:** David Gowans. 58-59 **Dreamstime.com:** Severija (t).
58 **Dorling Kindersley:** Wallace Collection, London (l). 59 **Dorling Kindersley:** Wallace Collection, London.
60-61 **Dreamstime.com:** Severija (t) *Endpapers:* **Dorling Kindersley:** Courtesy of the Wallace Collection, London.
Jacket images: *Front:* **Alamy Images:** CW Images, Seymour Rogansky tr; **Dorling Kindersley:** Board of Trustees of
the Royal Armouries cra, Pitt Rivers Museum, University of Oxford ca, Wallace Collection, London crb, bc,
Warwick Castle, Warwick cra/ (hammer); **Dreamstime.com:** Vladimirs Poplavskis / Fxquadro l; *Back:* **Dorling
Kindersley:** Wallace Collection, London bc.

All other images © Dorling Kindersley
For further information see: www.dkimages.com

A WORLD OF IDEAS:
SEE ALL THERE IS TO KNOW
www.dk.com

Contents

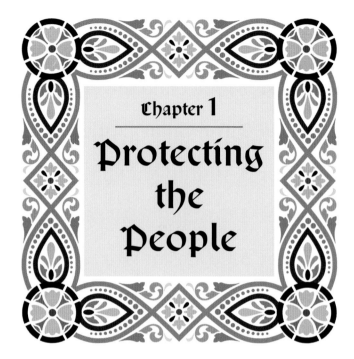

Chapter 1
Protecting the People

Castles were built to show power and protect people during times of trouble. When danger threatened, people took their **valuables** into the castle until the danger had ended. During a war, a castle would be filled with people from the nearby farms seeking protection. Even in peaceful times, castles provided protection from **bandits** and criminals.

Most castles were built in Europe between the years 950 and 1500. This period of time is often called the Middle Ages or Medieval Period. The design of castles changed over the years. As new weapons were invented to attack castles, the men building castles developed new methods of defence.

Carisbrooke Castle, England
First built over 900 years ago, this castle has had many changes.

Castles were often built on top of hills or beside rivers to make them more difficult to attack. Some castles were built beside a town to help defend it from enemies.

Early castles were made of wood and earth. A large mound of earth called a motte [MOT] was constructed up to 20 m (65 ft) tall and 60 m (200 ft) wide. On top of the motte was built a wooden tower. This was the strongest part of the castle.

Question

Where were castles often built and why were these sites chosen?

Beside the motte, a large area of ground was surrounded by a ditch and bank of earth. A wooden wall was built on top of the bank. This area was called the bailey. Several different buildings might be placed inside the bailey. Soldiers lived in barracks, while horses were kept in stables. The bailey might also include a church, offices, courthouse, workshops, kitchens or a great hall.

During peaceful times, castles were used for many different purposes. People went there to pay their **taxes** or to obtain justice from the courts. Criminals would be kept in prison inside castles. Valuable goods would be stored inside the storerooms. Over a hundred people might live inside a castle.

After about the year 1100, the wooden walls and towers began to be replaced with stone. Defences of stone were stronger and could not be set on fire so easily. Instead of a motte and tower, some castles had a massive square stone tower called a keep. The keep could be over 25 m (80 ft) tall. Soon new types of castle were being built.

Windsor Castle, England
The keep of this castle was rebuilt as the Round Tower in 1170.

Rochester Castle, England
Built in 1127, this tower keep has three floors.

Building a Motte-and-Bailey Castle

Things to Do List

1. Choose the site for the castle.

2. Hire a master builder to design the castle.

3. Hire 300 workmen to build the castle.

4. Buy enough timber to build the wooden walls and tower.

5. Dig the ditch around the bailey, and use the soil to construct the bank.

6. Build a wooden wall around the bailey.

7. Erect buildings in the bailey.

8. Dig a deep ditch around the motte, and pile up the soil to form the motte.

9. Build a tower on top of the motte.

10. Sit back and relax. You are safe from your enemies.

Chapter 2
The Great Castles

From about 1150, a new type of castle began to be built. Instead of earth and wood, the new castles were made of stone. They were the greatest castles ever built.

The new castles had stone walls that were tall enough to stop attackers on ladders reaching the top. The walls were so thick that missiles thrown at them from **catapults** had no effect.

Scaliger Castle, Italy
From the top of these thick, high walls, guards could see across Lake Garda.

On top of the walls were **crenellations** [KREN-el-lay-tions]. Defenders could hide behind the tall parts of the wall, or use their weapons through the gaps in between. Holes under the crenellations allowed defenders to drop heavy stones onto attackers below.

The walls had tall narrow holes in them called arrowslits. Guards standing inside could shoot bows through the arrowslits. The arrowslits were narrow to stop attackers shooting arrows back through them. Some arrowslits had a short **horizontal** slit to allow the guard inside a better view of the attackers.

Question

Why were arrowslits narrow?

The gate in the outer wall was guarded by a gatehouse. A tall tower protected each side of the gate. A heavy grid of wood called a **portcullis** [port-KULL-is] could be dropped to block the gateway.

A wooden platform called a drawbridge might cover a pit in front of the gate. The drawbridge was lifted when the gate was closed.

Sometimes a **barbican** was built outside the gatehouse. This building was like a small castle with walls and towers. Enemies had to capture the barbican before they could attack the gatehouse.

Many castles were surrounded by a deep **trench** called a moat. Some moats were flooded with water from a nearby stream or spring.

Later castles had lower walls outside higher walls. These are known as **concentric** [con-SEN-tric] castles. Guards on the inner walls could shoot arrows over the lower walls at the enemy. If the attackers captured the outer walls, they were overlooked by the inner walls.

Caerphilly [CAR-filly] **Castle, Wales**
Built between 1268 and 1271, this is the earliest concentric castle in the UK.

Most castles had one tower that was taller and had thicker walls than the others. This was the keep or donjon [dun-jun]. It was the strongest part of the castle and would be the last section to be captured by attackers.

The high inner wall was surrounded by a low outer wall.

Cool Castles

Many impressive castles and castle ruins can be visited across Europe and the Middle East. Here are just a few. Which castles would you add to this list?

Tower of London, England

The White Tower was built by William the Conqueror in 1078. It served as a keep as well as a home.

Krak des Chevaliers, Syria

This Arab fortress on a hilltop was rebuilt into a great, imposing castle between 1142 and 1271.

Château de Vincennes, France

This royal fortress in a forest had a donjon tower built around 1337. It is 52 m (170 ft) high.

Château Gaillard, France

Built in the year 1196, this castle was attacked many times, and also used as a prison.

Rocca Calascio, Italy

A mountaintop watchtower was turned into this impenetrable fortress in the 1200s.

Segovia Alcazar, Spain

Built on a rocky crag above two rivers, this castle has been a fortress, a palace and a prison.

Harlech, Wales

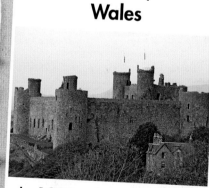

In 1280s, this was one of many castles built around Wales by an English King to show his control.

Come and Live in **Bodíam**

Sir Edward Dalyngrigge has now finished building Bodiam Castle. The soldiers living in the castle protect the Rother Valley from attack by the French. Your farm, family and property will be safe.

Good farmland at cheap prices. Total safety from French attack.

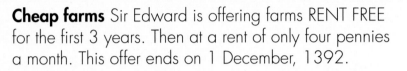

Cheap farms Sir Edward is offering farms RENT FREE for the first 3 years. Then at a rent of only four pennies a month. This offer ends on 1 December, 1392.

Good land The Rother Valley has good soil for corn, hops and cattle. You will be able to grow good crops.

Fast transport Your land will be close to the main road from Hastings to London.

Sign up now!

Chapter 3

Mighty Knights

In 1329, King Robert of Scotland lay dying. One of his last requests was to ask his loyal and brave knight, Sir James Douglas, to carry his heart on Crusade. Over the past 23 years, they had fought many a battle together. Their greatest victory came in 1314 when they defeated the English at the Battle of Bannockburn.

Together with 11 other knights, Sir James went to Spain to fight against the **Moors**. He carried the king's heart in a silver necklace. He was killed leading a charge at the Battle of Teba in August 1330. His body and the king's heart were taken back to Scotland for burial.

**Robert
the Bruce**
(1274–1329)

During the Middle Ages, when castles were built, society was divided into three groups: the farmers and craft workers, the priests and bishops, and the king and his knights. The knights were organised in a strict order of importance. Squires were training to be knights, while bannerets were senior knights.

All knights were expected to obey a code of behaviour known as chivalry [SHIV-al-ree]. Knights had to be brave in battle, but gentle in peace. They were supposed to protect the innocent and punish the guilty, and be especially kind to women and children. Knights were expected to serve their king faithfully and respect the Church and God's teachings.

Sir John Chandos (c.1314–1370)
Although not very good at fighting, Sir John
was highly skilled at organising an army.

Some knights were not born into nobility. John Hawkwood was the son of a **tanner** in Essex. In about 1340, he became a soldier and joined the English army invading France. In 1356, he fought so well at the Battle of Poitiers [PWA-ty-ay] that the King of England, Edward III, made him a knight.

When peace was arranged between England and France, Hawkwood formed a private army of unemployed soldiers. Named the "White Company", he marched them into Italy, and his army was hired out to whichever nobleman would pay him the most money. Hawkwood and his men made huge sums of money, and he married a wealthy duke's daughter.

◀ **Sir John Hawkwood** (c.1320–1394)
This is Sir John's **funerary** monument in Florence Cathedral, Italy.

"El Cid", meaning "The Lord", was the nickname of a heroic Spanish knight, Rodrigo Diaz de Vivar. He was born in 1040 into a noble family in the kingdom of Castile. In 1065, King Sancho of Spain made El Cid his **standard** bearer. Carrying the flag, El Cid bravely and skillfully led the army into battle, fighting against the Moors of southern Spain.

However in 1081, the new king, Alfonso, quarrelled with El Cid and sent him into **exile**. El Cid captured the Spanish city of Valencia [va-LEN-see-ah] in 1094 and declared himself ruler. When he was killed in battle in 1099, his wife had his body strapped to his horse so he could lead one last charge.

Rodrigo Diaz de Vivar ▶
(c.1040–1099)

Tall Tale

In 1357, a book was published called *The Travels of Sir John Mandeville*.
The book is claimed to be written by an English knight who had visited Turkey, Armenia, Persia, Syria, Arabia, Egypt, Libya, Ethiopia, Chaldea, India, Jerusalem, Indonesia, China and eastern Asia.

Why was the book a sensation?
Nobody had ever travelled to so many places or seen such exciting things. In Asia, Sir John met a race of humans who had only one leg and a gigantic foot on which they hopped around.

He also met people with horses' hooves instead of feet, and others who had their heads beneath their shoulders instead of on top.

Was the book true or untrue?
People at first believed that Sir John really had visited all the places he included. It was only later that people realised that much of the book was untrue. The sections about Europe and the Middle East were true, but the rest was not.

Why did Sir John invent some of it?
Maybe to make his book more exciting, or maybe somebody else added them later. We will never know.

Sir William Marshal's CV

Name: Sir William Marshal

Nationality: English

Year of birth: 1146, Wiltshire

Early profession: rode around Europe fighting in tournaments and working as a soldier for nobles, earls and dukes.

Achievements: from humble beginnings as son of a poor English knight, became so successful in tournaments that by 1189 was one of the richest men in Europe.

Titles: married Isabel de Clare, Countess of Pembroke.
1190 Knight at the King's Council
1216 Regent of England for the nine-year-old King Henry III
Ruled England until death in 1219.

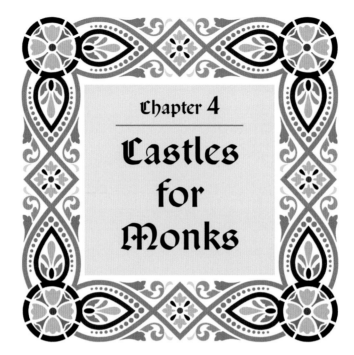

Chapter 4

Castles for Monks

Some castles were built for an unusual group of monks, who fought like knights. They were called the Military Orders of Monks.

In 1119, the French knight Sir Hugues de Payens found the bodies of a group of **pilgrims** near Jerusalem. They had been murdered by bandits on their way to the holy city.

Sir Hugues founded a group of fighting monks called The Poor Fellow Soldiers of Christ. Their job was to patrol the roads to protect the pilgrims. King Baldwin of Jerusalem gave buildings on the Temple Mount in the city to them, and these monk-knights became known as the Knights Templar. For 200 years, they built castles, including the huge Kerak Castle, and fought battles in the Holy Land (now Israel).

Kerak Castle, Jordan
Begun in 1132, it has cliffs on two sides.

About the year 1120, the monks of the Order of St. John of the Hospital also took up arms to protect pilgrims to help them reach the holy sites. These Knights Hospitaller built many impressive castles to defend the route. Rebuilt in 1186, Margat Castle with its round towers perched on top of cliffs became their greatest castle.

The Knights Hospitaller also had a navy to protect pilgrims travelling by sea from attacks by pirates. They

Margat Castle, Syria
Also known as Marqab, this castle was triangular shaped with a steep drop on one side.

built castles on islands along the Mediterranean Sea as command posts such as Kolossi Castle on Cyprus in 1254. They later ruled Malta until 1798, and today they are based in Rome.

Kolossi Castle, Cyprus
Just one large tower now remains.

In 1190, the Order of Teutonic [too-TON-ic] Knights was founded in Germany to protect pilgrims travelling to the Holy Land. In 1220, these knights bought the village of Mi'ilya and built Castellum Regis with its four massive square towers and a small church inside. In 1229, a tall narrow ridge became the site of their **headquarters** in the Holy Land, Montfort Castle.

Malbork Castle, Poland has been enlarged several times and now covers 52 acres, making it the world's largest castle.

From 1230 onwards, the Teutonic Knights fought wars against the non-Christians in eastern Europe to protect Christian Germany. Malbork Castle, now in Poland, was built in 1274 as their world headquarters. By 1400, the threat had disappeared so the order became involved in charity work instead.

As well as the three great Military Orders, there were lots of smaller ones. The Order of Aviz was founded in 1146 to protect the Kingdom of Portugal against

Beaufort Castle, Lebanon
Called the "Beautiful Castle", Beaufort was held by the Knights Templar until 1268.

the Moors. The Order of Calatrava fought to re-conquer Spain from the Moors from 1164 to 1490. The Order of the Dragon

was founded in Hungary in 1408 to fight the Turks.

All these Military Orders had a large role in the Crusades. These were expeditions by armies from medieval Europe to the Holy Land to fight against the Turks. Small forts such as Saone [SONE] Castle in Syria were rebuilt into huge, strong castles by the crusaders.

Saone Castle, Syria

Saone Castle is thought to be one of the strongest castles in the world, but in 1188 it fell after a siege of just three days.

Crusade Preparations

 1 Announce you are going on Crusade.

 2 Ask for volunteers to join you.

 3 Ask for money to pay for the Crusade.

 4 Meet the volunteers. Check their weapons and armour.

 5 Count how much money you have collected.

6 Buy flags and clothing for your army.

7 Decide where you are going to attack.

8 Hire ships to take your army on Crusade.

9 March your army to the docks.

10 Set off for your Crusade.

Good Luck!

Chapter 5

Castles at War

In 1136, Sir Baldwin de Redvers, Earl of Devon, rebelled against King Stephen of England. The king marched his army to lay **siege** [SEE-j] to Sir Baldwin's castle in Exeter. The king's army built a wooden castle to protect them, and surrounded Exeter Castle to block supplies reaching Sir Baldwin and his people. The attackers used siege weapons to smash the walls of

What actions did the king's army take to lay siege to Exeter Castle?

the outer bailey. They also dug a tunnel under the East Tower, causing it to collapse. Sir Baldwin finally surrendered after dry weather caused the well to go dry.

When a siege took place, a castle became a very busy place. Hundreds of people from nearby farms and villages would come to the castle for safety, bringing their belongings. Tents and sheds were put up in the bailey along with large numbers of farm animals, carts and tools.

The knight who owned the castle had to prepare for a siege. He brought huge amounts of food into the castle's storerooms. He made sure his soldiers had plenty of weapons and equipment. Riders on fast horses were sent out to look for the enemy approaching. When the enemy was seen, the gate was locked shut. No one could leave and no further supplies could come in. The soldiers manned the walls, ready to fight.

Supplying provisions
This picture on a manuscript from the 1300s shows supplies arriving at a castle.

The siege of Kenilworth Castle lasted longer than most. It began in January 1266 when King Henry III attacked rebels led by Henry de Hastings. The wide moat surrounding the castle meant that  the king's siege towers were useless and the catapults' stones could not reach the castle walls.

King Henry brought barges to carry his army over the moat, but they were sunk by the defenders of the castle. An effort to cross the water by raft also failed. Finally an **envoy** from the Pope in Rome arranged a peace deal and the rebels surrendered in December 1266.

Kenilworth Castle, England
This castle later became a splendid palace in the 1500s.

Neither side wanted a siege to last long, but both wanted to win. In 1341, Scottish nobleman William Douglas set out to attack Edinburgh Castle, which was being held by the English. One night, Douglas led 1,000 men to hide in trees near the castle. At dawn, 20 men pretending to be merchants drove a wagon to the castle. They said they brought food to sell.

Edinburgh Castle, Scotland
This castle was built on a tall
volcanic crag.

The English opened the gates to let
the "merchants" in. Dozens of Scottish
soldiers were hiding in the cart. They
leapt out to defend the gate and keep
it open until Douglas arrived with his
army to burst in and capture the castle.

Grim Discovery at Dolforwyn

A gruesome find has been uncovered by scientists at Dolforwyn Castle in Powys.

Archaeologists carrying out the dig are baffled. Archaeologist Daniel Mersey says, "A horse skull and neck bones were found embedded in the castle's north wall."

The find came as archaeologists were digging around the base of the huge D-shaped tower in the north wall. It was the fourth year that scientists have worked at Dolforwyn.

Mr. Mersey continued, "Behind the D-shaped tower, I uncovered a vaulted cellar. The closed end of the cellar has a small hole. We found metalwork by this, which may well have been from a trapdoor. The cellar was probably the wine cellar known to have existed, and other metal strips may be from storage barrels."

Dolforwyn Castle, recently excavated ruins in Powys, Wales.

The horse's head was found lodged inside a wall beside the cellar. Nobody knows why the skull is there. The castle was built in 1273 by a Welsh prince. It was abandoned in about 1400. The finds from the excavation are being preserved by the Cadw [CAD-wuh] organisation and may be put on display in Cardiff Museum in Wales.

Siege of Harlech
(1461-68)

The defences of Harlech Castle were so strong that the attackers decided not to attack, but to try to starve the garrison into surrender. Supplies, however, could reach the castle by sea. The seven-year long siege only ended when an army of 10,000 well-armed men attacked and the outer defences fell. The defenders of Harlech are remembered in this song.

Song Lyrics

Hark! I hear the foe advancing,
Barbed steeds are proudly prancing,
Helmets in the sunbeams glancing
Glitter through the trees.
Men of Harlech, lie ye dreaming?

Knights and Castles Quiz

1. What was used to make early castles?

2. What was the strongest part of a castle?

3. Who carried King Robert of Scotland's heart on Crusade?

4. How did Sir William Marshal become rich?

5. Which Military Order of monks used Margat Castle?

Answers on page 61.

Glossary

bandits
group of robbers or people who break the law

barbican
tower and walls that form an outer defence of a castle

catapult
weapon that throws large stones

concentric
circles of different sizes with the same centre

crenellations
battlements with regular gaps

envoy
messenger or representative

exile
unable to live in own country

funerary
used to remember a dead person

headquarters
main offices from where an organisation is controlled

horizontal
flat or level, going from side to side

Moors
group of people with African and Arab ancestry

pilgrims
religious people who travel to a sacred place

portcullis

strong, heavy gate made from iron or wooden bars with points at the bottom, which hangs over a gateway into a castle

siege

when an enemy surrounds a town or building, cutting off supplies and trying to force those inside to surrender

standard

flag of a royal family

tanner

person whose job is to make animal skins into leather

taxes

payment that has to be made to those in authority

trench

long, narrow hole dug out in the ground

valuables

small objects, such as jewellery, that belong to someone, and are worth a lot to them

---

Answers to Knights and Castles Quiz:
1. Wood and earth; 2. Keep or donjon;
3. Sir James Douglas; 4. Fighting in tournaments;
5. Knights Hospitaller.

Guide for Parents

DK Readers is a four-level interactive reading adventure series for children, developing the habit of reading widely for both pleasure and information. These chapter books have an exciting main narrative interspersed with a range of reading genres to suit your child's reading ability, as required by the National Curriculum. Each book is designed to develop your child's reading skills, fluency, grammar awareness, and comprehension in order to build confidence and engagement when reading.

Ready for a *Beginning to Read Alone* book

YOUR CHILD SHOULD

- be able to read most words without needing to stop and break them down into sound parts.
- read smoothly, in phrases and with expression. By this level, your child will be mostly reading silently.
- self-correct when some word or sentence doesn't sound right.

A VALUABLE AND SHARED READING EXPERIENCE

For some children, text reading, particularly non-fiction, requires much effort but adult participation can make this both fun and easier. So here are a few tips on how to use this book with your child.

TIP 1 Check out the contents together before your child begins:

- invite your child to check the blurb, contents page and layout of the book and comment on it.
- ask your child to make predictions about the story.
- chat about the information your child might want to find out.

TIP 2 Encourage fluent and flexible reading:

- support your child to read in fluent, expressive phrases, making full use of punctuation and thinking about the meaning.

- encourage your child to slow down and check information where appropriate.

TIP 3 Indicators that your child is reading for meaning:

- your child will be responding to the text if he/she is self-correcting and varying his/her voice.
- your child will want to talk about what he/she is reading or is eager to turn the page to find out what will happen next.

TIP 4 Praise, share and chat:

- the factual pages tend to be more difficult than the story pages, and are designed to be shared with your child.
- encourage your child to recall specific details after each chapter.
- provide opportunities for your child to pick out interesting words and discuss what they mean.
- discuss how the author captures the reader's interest, or how effective the non-fiction layouts are.
- ask questions about the text. These help to develop comprehension skills and awareness of the language used.

A FEW ADDITIONAL TIPS

- Read to your child regularly to demonstrate fluency, phrasing and expression; to find out or check information; and for sharing enjoyment.
- Encourage your child to reread favourite texts to increase reading confidence and fluency.
- Check that your child is reading a range of different types, such as poems, jokes and following instructions.

Index